Your Homemade Sanitizer

The Best Homemade Sanitizer Recipes for a Healthier Lifestyle

BY

Jenny Kings

License Notes

No part of this Book can be reproduced in any form or by any means including print, electronic, scanning or photocopying unless prior permission is granted by the author.

All ideas, suggestions and guidelines mentioned here are written for informative purposes. While the author has taken every possible step to ensure accuracy, all readers are advised to follow information at their own risk. The author cannot be held responsible for personal and/or commercial damages in case of misinterpreting and misunderstanding any part of this Book

Homemade Sanitizer

Recipes

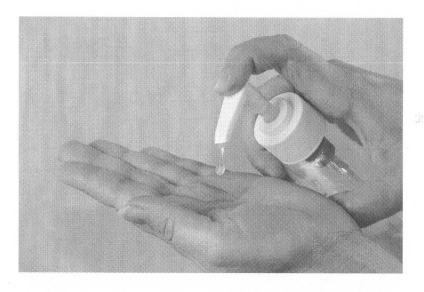

Table of Contents

DIY Hand Sanitizer Gel

Recipes

ooooooooooooooooooooooooooooooooooooooo

(1) Lemon Oil Gel Recipe

Many people love the fragrance of lemon which makes them feel refreshing. Here is the awesome recipe for hand sanitizer with the lemon aroma.

List of Ingredients:

- Rubbing alcohol – 1 tablespoon
- Aloe Vera gel – ½ tablespoons
- Lemon essential oil – 5 drops
- Tea tree oil – 5 drops
- Water (filtered) – 2 cups

OO

Instructions:

To make the gel hand sanitizer, mix all the ingredients together such as rubbing alcohol, aloe Vera gel, lemon oil, tea tree oil and water. Blend it well and then use it whenever you want to clean your hands.

(2) Sweet Orange Flavor Gel

Sweet orange flavor hand sanitizer gel makes you feel energetic with its smell and keeps your mood happy.

List of Ingredients:

- Rubbing alcohol – 1 tablespoon
- Aloe Vera gel – ½ tablespoons
- Sweet Orange essential oil – 15 drops
- Tea tree oil – 5 drops
- Water (filtered) – 2 cups

OOOOOOOOOOOOOOOOOOOOOOOOOOOOOOOOOOOOOOOOOO

Instructions:

To make the gel hand sanitizer, mix all the ingredients together such as rubbing alcohol, aloe Vera gel, sweet orange oil, tea tree oil and water. Blend it well and then use it whenever you want to clean your hands.

(3) Chamomile Oil Gel

The yellow flower gives you a beautiful feel of flower in your hands with this awesome recipe.

List of Ingredients:

- Rubbing alcohol – 2 tablespoons
- Aloe Vera gel – ½ tablespoons
- Chamomile essential oil – 10 drops
- Tea tree oil – 5 drops
- Water (filtered) – 2 cups

oooooooooooooooooooooooooooooooooooooooooo

Instructions:

To make the gel hand sanitizer, mix all the ingredients together such as rubbing alcohol, aloe Vera gel, chamomile oil, tea tree oil and water. Blend it well and then use it whenever you want to clean your hands.

(4) Essential Oils Gel Hand Sanitizer

rather than using a commercial hand sanitizer, why not try the natural gel sanitizer at home and that too made of herbal.

List of Ingredients:

- Aloe Vera gel – ¼ cup
- Orange essential oil – 20 drops
- Clove essential oil – 5 drops
- Cinnamon essential oil – 10 drops
- Lavender essential oil – 10 drops
- Rosemary essential oil – 5 drops

OOOOOOOOOOOOOOOOOOOOOOOOOOOOOOOOOOOOOOOOOO

Instructions:

Mix all the following ingredients together such as aloe Vera gel, orange essential oil, clove essential oil, cinnamon oil, lavender oil and rosemary oil. Blend it well and then pour it in a bottle. It will form in a texture of gel, and you can use it as hygiene.

(5) Frankincense Oil Gel Hand Sanitizer

Get the best germ-killing hand sanitizer recipe along with mesmerizing aroma in your hands.

List of Ingredients:

- Rubbing alcohol – 1 tablespoon
- Aloe Vera gel – ½ tablespoons
- Frankincense essential oil – 10 drops
- Tea tree oil – 5 drops
- Water (filtered) – 2 cups

oooooooooooooooooooooooooooooooooooooo

Instructions:

To make the gel hand sanitizer, mix all the ingredients together such as rubbing alcohol, aloe Vera gel, frankincense oil, tea tree oil and water. Blend it well and then use it whenever you want to clean your hands.

(6) Cinnamon Flavor Gel Recipe

A natural recipe of gel hand sanitizer is all you need to get started with the hygiene when you are not at home.

List of Ingredients:

- Rubbing alcohol – 1 tablespoon
- Aloe Vera gel – ½ tablespoons
- Cinnamon essential oil – 5 drops
- Tea tree oil – 5 drops
- Water (filtered) – 2 cups

OOO

Instructions:

To make the gel hand sanitizer, mix all the ingredients together such as rubbing alcohol, aloe Vera gel, cinnamon oil, tea tree oil and water. Blend it well and then use it whenever you want to clean your hands.

(7) Peppermint Aroma Gel

Peppermint gives energy to the mind and body, apply this hand sanitizer, and you will be fresh again.

List of Ingredients:

- Rubbing alcohol – 1 tablespoon
- Aloe Vera gel – ½ tablespoons
- Peppermint essential oil – 15 drops
- Tea tree oil – 5 drops
- Water (filtered) – 2 cups

OO

Instructions:

To make the gel hand sanitizer, mix all the ingredients together such as rubbing alcohol, aloe Vera gel, peppermint oil, tea tree oil and water. Blend it well and then use it whenever you want to clean your hands.

(8) Beautiful Lavender Hand Sanitizer Gel

The recipe of hand sanitizer gels not just cleans but leaves a beautiful aroma of lavender in your hands.

List of Ingredients:

- Rubbing alcohol – 2 tablespoons
- Aloe Vera gel – ½ tablespoons
- Lavender essential oil – 20 drops
- Tea tree oil – 5 drops
- Water (filtered) – 2 cups

OOOOOOOOOOOOOOOOOOOOOOOOOOOOOOOOOOOOOOOOOOOO

Instructions:

To make the gel hand sanitizer, mix all the ingredients together such as rubbing alcohol, aloe Vera gel, lavender oil, tea tree oil and water. Blend it well and then use it whenever you want to clean your hands.

(9) Rosemary Aroma Gel

Just smelling the rosemary makes you feel happy, how about applying the hand sanitizer made of it?

List of Ingredients:

- Rubbing alcohol – 2 tablespoons
- Aloe Vera gel – ½ tablespoons
- Rosemary essential oil – 15 drops
- Tea tree oil – 5 drops
- Water (filtered) – 2 cups

OO

Instructions:

To make the gel hand sanitizer, mix all the ingredients together such as rubbing alcohol, aloe Vera gel, rosemary oil, tea tree oil and water. Blend it well and then use it whenever you want to clean your hands.

(10) Clove Essential Oil Gel Recipe

Clove is the ingredients which work as healing for the body. Try this recipe to get rid of germs and clean your hands completely.

List of Ingredients:

- Rubbing alcohol – 2 tablespoons
- Aloe Vera gel – ½ tablespoons
- Clove essential oil – 20 drops
- Tea tree oil – 5 drops
- Water (filtered) – 2 cups

ooooooooooooooooooooooooooooooooooooooo

Instructions:

To make the gel hand sanitizer, mix all the ingredients together such as rubbing alcohol, aloe Vera gel, clove oil, tea tree oil and water. Blend it well and then use it whenever you want to clean your hands.

DIY Hand Sanitizer Spray Recipes

ooooooooooooooooooooooooooooooooooooooooooo

(11) Vegetable Glycerin Spray Recipe

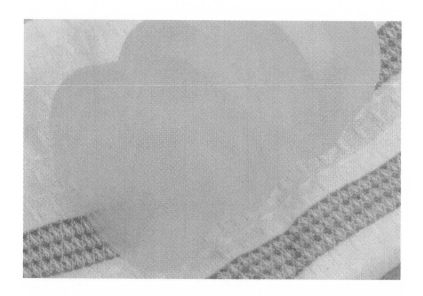

This recipe does not only kills the germs of your hands but makes it smell beautiful as well.

List of Ingredients:

- Aloe Vera gel – ¼ cup
- Rubbing alcohol – ¾ cup
- Vegetable glycerin – 1/8 cup
- Cinnamon oil – 10 drops
- Sweet orange oil – 10 drops

OO

Instructions:

Get a food processor and add all the ingredients such as aloe Vera gel, rubbing alcohol, vegetable glycerin, cinnamon oil and sweet orange oil in it. Blend it well and then pour it into the spray bottle. Now whenever you need, you will have the homemade sanitizer to clean your hands.

(12) Antiseptic Spray

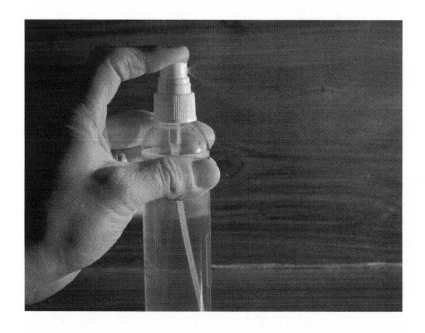

Antiseptic spray is made of essential oils which do not only clean your skin but also makes it smooth.

List of Ingredients:

- Witch Hazel – 1 tablespoon
- Aloe Vera gel – 2 tablespoons
- Vitamin E oil – 2 teaspoons
- Lavender oil– 10 drops
- Tea tree oil – 10 drops
- Frankincense oil – 10 drops
- Water – 2 cups

OOOOOOOOOOOOOOOOOOOOOOOOOOOOOOOOOOOOOOOO

Instructions:

Mix all the ingredients together such as witch hazel, aloe Vera gel, vitamin E oil, Lavender oil, tea tree oil and frankincense oil in a bottle. Then add water in it and shake it well. Cover it and let it store for a bit, after a while spray the sanitizer and enjoy the hygiene.

(13) Vitamin E Oil Spray

Best combination of essential oils which makes your hands clean and leaves the skin moisturized as well.

List of Ingredients:

- Vitamin E oil – 5 drops
- Tea tree oil – 5 drops
- Aloe Vera Gel – 3 tablespoons
- Dispenser tube
- Water (filtered) – 2 cups

OOOOOOOOOOOOOOOOOOOOOOOOOOOOOOOOOOOOOOOOOO

Instructions:

Mix all the ingredients together such as water, aloe Vera gel, tea tree oil and vitamin E oil. Shake it well in the dispenser tube and then use it as a sanitizer spray for your hands.

(14) Pure Aloe Vera Spray

Treat yourself with the soft scent of natural essence using this hand sanitizer recipe

List of Ingredients:

- Lavender essential oil – 5 drops
- Tea tree oil – 5 drops
- Pure Aloe Vera Gel – 8 ounces
- Hazel extract – 1 tablespoon
- Vitamin E oil – ¼ teaspoons

OOO

Instructions:

Mix the lavender oil and vitamin E oil together in a bowl and while stirring it, add the hazel extract along with the tea tree oil. When it is all blend completely, then add the aloe Vera gel into it. Add it in a bottle and then mix well every time you want to use it. Preferably, it should be the spray bottle.

(15) Ethyl Alcohol recipe

Alcohol is essential to kill all the germs which are present on your hands. It does not harm the skin at all so try this recipe now.

List of Ingredients:

- Ethyl Alcohol – 1 tablespoon
- Vitamin E oil – 2 teaspoons
- Aloe Vera gel – 2 teaspoons
- Sweet orange oil – 10 drops
- Water (filtered) - 1 cup

OOOOOOOOOOOOOOOOOOOOOOOOOOOOOOOOOOOOOOOOOOOO

Instructions:

Mix all the ingredients together such as ethyl alcohol, vitamin E oil, Aloe Vera gel, sweet orange oil, and water. Shake it well in the bottle and then use it as a spray.

(16) The Natural Spray recipe

The natural recipe of simple hand sanitizer will allow you to avoid alcohol in it.

List of Ingredients:

- Water – 2 tablespoons
- Witch hazel – 2 tablespoons
- Vegetable glycerin – 1 tablespoon
- Tea tree oil – 20 drops
- Lemongrass essential oil – 5 drops
- Rosemary essential oil – 5 drops

OOOOOOOOOOOOOOOOOOOOOOOOOOOOOOOOOOOOOOOOO

Instructions:

Get a bottle with the cap and the spray on it. Add water first and then combine all the following ingredients in it such as witch hazel, vegetable glycerin, tea tree oil, lemongrass oil and rosemary oil together. Blend it together. Spritz the spray on your hand for 2-3 times and then rub it together for it to dry.

DIY Hand Sanitizer Wipes

OOOOOOOOOOOOOOOOOOOOOOOOOOOOOOOOOOOOOOOOOOOO

(17) Tea Tree Oil Wipes

Quick and simple recipe to make the wipes with your favorite fragrance of tea tree oil.

List of Ingredients:

- Paper towel – 1 roll
- Plastic jar with lid – 1
- Water (filtered) – 1 cup
- Ethyl Alcohol – ¾ cup
- Tea tree oil – 40 drops

OOO

Instructions:

Cut the paper towels in half and keep it in a plastic jar. Now add the ingredients such as water, alcohol and tea tree oil. Keep it covered for a while and then take it out to be placed in a container or the Ziploc bag where the air cannot pass to make it dry.

(18) Lavender Oil Wipes Recipe

Try this perfect fragmented recipe to use the wipes with leaving the aroma around you.

List of Ingredients:

- Warm water – 1 cup
- Coconut oil – 1 tablespoon
- Vodka – 1 teaspoon
- Lavender oil – 3 drops
- Lemon oil – 3 drops

OOOOOOOOOOOOOOOOOOOOOOOOOOOOOOOOOOOOOOOOOOOO

Instructions:

Mix the coconut oil separate in the warm water and then soak the paper towels in it. Add the essential oils of lavender and lemon with vodka. Keep it covered in a Ziploc bag for 4 hours and then place it in a container so that it absorbs all the ingredients. You can use these to clean hands or any place such as carts, door knobs and much more.

(19) Home Made Hand Sanitizer Wipes

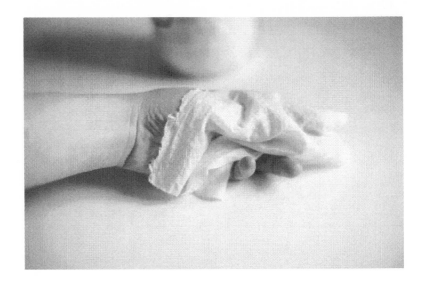

Wipes can be used to clean any area where you are about to put your hands or to clean your hands. Try this recipe to make at home.

List of Ingredients:

- Homemade lotion – 1 tablespoon
- Rubbing alcohol – 2 tablespoons
- Lavender essential oil – 15 drops
- Paper towels – 10
- Ziploc bag – 5
- Container for the finished wipes

OOOOOOOOOOOOOOOOOOOOOOOOOOOOOOOOOOOOOOOOO

Instructions:

Add the lavender oil, rubbing alcohol and homemade lotion into the Ziploc bag with placing a paper towel in it by folding it. Now keep it inside for about 4 hours and let it get absorbed. When it is all absorbed, take it out and place it in the container so that it stays wet and you can use it to clean your hands or any other place you wish to clean when you are outside of the home.

(20) Rubbing Alcohol Wipes

An easy to make a recipe for the wipes which you can make at home with no additional cost.

List of Ingredients:

- Paper towels – 1 roll
- Water – ½ cup
- Rubbing alcohol – ½ cup
- Aloe Vera – ¼ cup

OOOOOOOOOOOOOOOOOOOOOOOOOOOOOOOOOOOOOOOOOOO

Instructions:

Grab the paper towels and cut them in half. Put them in the container and then add the following ingredients to it such as rubbing alcohol, Aloe Vera and water in it. Check it after a while, and you can use it whenever you want as a wipe.

(21) Alcohol- Free wipes

If you do not want alcohol in the wipes, then here is the perfect homemade recipe for you!

List of Ingredients:

- Water (filtered) – ¼ cup
- Aloe Vera gel – ¼ cup
- Witch hazel – ¼ cup
- Apple cider vinegar – 1 tablespoon
- Vegetable glycerin – 1 tablespoon
- Tea tree oil – 10 drops
- Peppermint essential oil – 10 drops

OOO

Instructions:

Grab a stack of paper towels and a Ziploc bag, add all the following ingredients in it such as peppermint oil, tea tree oil, vegetable glycerin, aloe Vera gel, witch hazel, apple cider vinegar and then water in it. Let the paper towel get soaked in it and then place it in a container so that it stays wet and you can use it as a wipe whenever you have to.

(22) Sanitizer Wipes from Baby Wipes

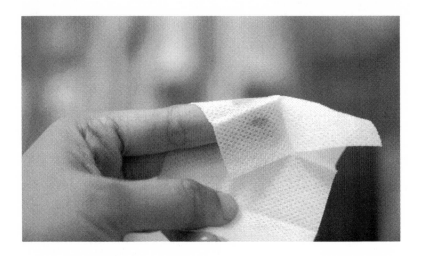

Baby wipes are not just for the babies, but you can make use of them for your hygiene as well. Try this recipe and keep your surroundings clean.

List of Ingredients:

- Unscented baby wipes
- Alcohol – 3 tablespoons
- Ziploc bag

ooooooooooooooooooooooooooooooooooooooo

Instructions:

Put the wipes in the Ziploc bag and then pour the tablespoons of Alcohol in the wipe. Shake it well so that the wipes catch the alcohol and cover it well. After a while, it will be saturated; then you can use these wipes as a sanitizer wipe for yourself by keeping it secure in a container.

(23) The Alcohol Version wipes

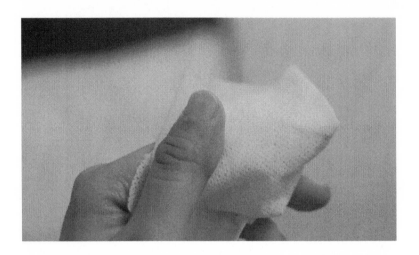

You think alcohol can clean the germs better? Then this is the right recipe for you.

List of Ingredients:

- Aloe Vera gel – ½ cup
- Water (filtered) – ¼ cup
- Rubbing alcohol – ¼ cup
- Witch hazel – 1 tablespoon
- Cinnamon essential oil – 20 drops

ooooooooooooooooooooooooooooooooooooooooooo

Instructions:

Get a bunch of paper towels and cut them in half. Roll them in a stack and then add the following ingredients in a Ziploc bag such as witch hazel, cinnamon essential oil, water, rubbing alcohol and aloe Vera gel. Let the paper towel absorb all the mixture and then when the paper towels smell beautiful then place it in a box where you can keep it wet to use it later.

DIY Hand Sanitizer Holder

OOOOOOOOOOOOOOOOOOOOOOOOOOOOOOOOOOOOOOOO

(24) Fabric Made Hand Sanitizer Holder

A protective shield holder for your hand sanitizer is just a few steps away with these awesome directions.

Material:

- Bottle of hand sanitizer
- Fabrics – 10 inches long
- Iron-on interface – 10 inches long
- Elastic – 1 inch long (color of your choice)
- Button – ½ inch wide
- Needle – 1

OOOOOOOOOOOOOOOOOOOOOOOOOOOOOOOOOOOOOOOOO

Instructions:

Cut the fabric according to the size of the hand sanitizer bottle. Now you can decide which side you want to keep up. Work on the right side of it first and then connect the midline with both shell fabric and the lining fabric. Elastic should be marked from both ends and make it short opening from the front. Insert the button on the edge which should be parallel to the bottle. Now fix the hand sanitizer bottle in it with hanging it anywhere you want.

You can simply open the button to release the bottle to the front to make use of the sanitizer. It will keep it safe, and you won't have to look inside your bag which will consume your time.

(25) Home Made Holder

Get a hold of hand sanitizer anywhere you are and hand it with your key chain so you can access it easily anytime.

Material:

- Hair tie – 1
- Lobster clip – 1 (mini)
- Ribbon – 4 inches

OOOOOOOOOOOOOOOOOOOOOOOOOOOOOOOOOOOOOOOOO

Instructions:

Take the hair tie and knot it with the lobster clip. Make sure the knot it tied strong. Now cut the ribbon into 2 inches piece each and seal the ends. Sew them both together from a tube and then shut the ends. You can hang it with your keychains and whenever you need it, simply take out your keys and use the hand sanitizer along with it to kill the unseen germs on your hands.

Author's Afterthoughts

Thank you for reading my book. Your feedback is important to me. It would be greatly appreciated if you could please take a moment to REVIEW this book on Amazon so that we could make our next version better

Thanks!

Jenny Kings

Made in the USA
Monee, IL
17 March 2020